I Am Me Wherever I Go!

I Am Me Wherever I Go!

Published by Gatekeeper Press
2167 Stringtown Rd, Suite 109
Columbus, OH 43123-2989
www.GatekeeperPress.com

Library of Congress Control Number: 2021948601

ISBN (hardcover): 9781662917745
ISBN (paperback): 9781662917752
eISBN: 9781662917769

I Am Me
Wherever I Go!

Deidre Boyle

Illustrator: Veronica Giglia

gatekeeper press
Columbus, Ohio

AL'S
Sam's Deli
5th St.
Pizza
Bob's
321 CBA

We left the city to move to the suburbs. We now live in a house with a backyard. I even have my own room. The street is so nice with flowers, green lawns, and beautiful trees everywhere. It is amazing to see that every house has at least one car.

In the city, we lived in an apartment, and we walked everywhere. If we were going far, we would take the bus or the subway.

Things are so very different here. Will I be able to fit in?

Carnival
Park
GARDEN
VINNY'S DELI
'S SHOP
TOM'S
NEWSSTAND
FOOD
OPEN

I do not look like everyone here. In my old neighborhood, I looked like everyone else. I do not know how I will fit in. I do not have a bike. In this town, all the kids ride bikes up and down the streets. They ride them to the parks, and I heard that some kids even ride them to school.

Things are so very different here. Will I be able to fit in?

12
3
6
9
BANK
YOUR
AD
HERE!
321
SLOW

I woke up this morning to birds chirping. I did not hear any cars honking or trucks driving by on the street. When I heard a new and unusual sound, my mom explained that it was a lawnmower. I heard other lawn tools and machines, too. These sounds were all new to me because we didn't even have grass in the city.

Things are so very different here. Will I be able to fit in?

LOOP
MALL
TAXI
PETS
LOU'S FOOD
TOY SALE
2 FLOORS
Brian's Comics
OPEN
OPEN
1 $1
Suki's
DRESS SALE
Ron's Furni
SALE

Now, when my family and I go out on the weekends we sit in so much traffic. We must drive everywhere. The stores and shops are too far away to walk. In the city, we just walked down the block to shop, eat, and see all our friends.

Things are so very different here. Will I be able to fit in?

456
678

In the city, when my parents got home from work or on the weekends, we would walk to restaurants. Like us, all my friends and their families sat outside their apartments until it was time for bed. Here, there are no people out after dinner. On the weekends I hear people, but they are in their backyards.

Things are so very different here. Will I be able to fit in?

School will be starting soon, and I wonder what it will be like. Will that be very different too?

Will I make new friends? Will I fit in?

I am scared because everything is SO VERY DIFFERENT!

afe
BIKES
Le
OPEN
DELI
BAGELS
Lemonade
50¢

Today my family got invited to a block party. I know what that is. We had them in my old neighborhood. All the people were putting their lawn furniture in the street. They had a D.J. and a water slide. Everyone was so nice, and we had so much fun.

Maybe it is not so different. Maybe they are more like me than I thought.

SCHOOL

Today is my first day of school. All the kids I met at the block party asked me to play with them, and they introduced me to more new friends.

Maybe things are not so very different!

6 September
S M T W TH F S
We co

My teacher introduced herself to me and my family. As I looked at my class, I saw kids who looked like me and my friends in the city.

Things are not so different here.

I came home from school so happy. My mom asked me how my school day went, and I said it was a lot like my old school. My mom told me the teacher wants parents to feel included in school. My teacher has a sheet asking her to share about our family, special celebrations, parents' jobs, and anything else we want to share that makes us unique. The teacher explained that she has daily meetings with the class so they can learn about each other.

The teacher said parents, family members, or special people can sign up for times to share these things over the computer. My mom said the teacher explained that everywhere we go, we will meet people and experience things that are different. However, if we are all able to share and grow together, we will be happy being ourselves.

Things are not so different here. I told my mom, "It is going to be a great year!"

Name
All About Me
Family
Family Facts
Traditions
Favorite Foods
What Makes Me Unique
Extra Facts